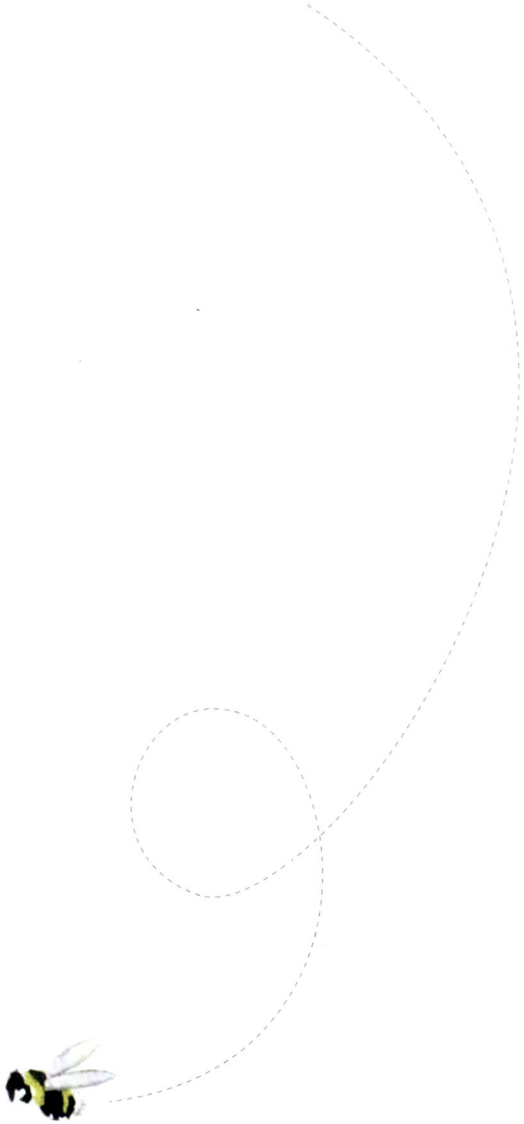

Character illustrations by Samantha Hanson.
Layout and additional artwork by Fiona Bowring.

Publisher: Independent Publishing Network.
Publication date: 2019
ISBN: 978-1-78972-222-2
Author: Ann Copeland
Distributor: www.inthegardenpoems.com
Enquiries: enquiries@inthegardenpoems.com

Copyright ©2013 Ann Copeland

All rights reserved. No part of this book may be reproduced in any form or by any electronic or mechanical means, including information storage and retrieval systems, without permission in writing from the distributor. Permission is not required by reviewers, who may quote brief passages in a review.

Please direct all book orders or enquiries to the distributor.

# Contents

| | |
|---|---|
| Daisy, Dale and Fred | 4 |
| Jerry Giraffe | 9 |
| The Little Frog | 13 |
| The Songbirds | 20 |
| The Humble Bumblebee | 24 |
| In My Garden | 27 |
| The Messages | 31 |
| About the Author | 32 |

# Introduction

This collection of children's poems is intended for children of all ages. I hope you find the poems entertaining and hopefully some of them funny. But besides their enjoyment value, you may consider it appropriate to tease out the sentiment that each poem is based on.

In some poems it might be obvious and for others perhaps a stretch of the imagination is needed. Whichever is the case, it might for someone, help start the voyage of discovery that hclps reveal both the content itself and the message embedded within most of what we read.

I have listed at the end of the book what I had in mind as I wrote each of the poems so that you can check to see whether your interpretation agrees with the messages I hope they convey.

I hope you enjoy reading my poems.

Ann Copeland

# Daisy, Dale and Fred

This little mouse whose name is Daisy
Is never one for being lazy,
She runs around the nest like crazy
This pretty mouse whose name is Daisy.

Then there's her brother who's known as Dale
With little ears and long thin tail,
Large pink eyes and skin so pale,
This younger mouse whose name is Dale.

And finally there's baby Fred
Who'd stay all day curled up in bed.
All you can see is his little head,
This baby mouse who they called Fred.

Each morning Daisy helps young Fred
To leave his warm and cosy bed.
She whispers, 'Come on sleepy head,
It's time we mice were washed and fed'.

Mother mouse has the table laid
With porridge, toast and marmalade.
The tea is brewed and cheese displayed
All neatly on a cloth that's frayed.

They live together without much bother
Daisy, Dale and their baby brother.
Three little mice with Dad and Mother
Taking care of one another.

# Jerry Giraffe

Jerry giraffe with the funny laugh
could eat from the tallest of trees.
His very big tongue was ever so strong
and could tear off the greenest of leaves.

One day as he chewed his freshly picked food a monkey told him a joke. He wanted to laugh, did Jerry giraffe, but he started to splutter and choke.

The monkey, in fright, threw his arms
quite tight round the neck of Jerry giraffe.
Then he started to slide and, enjoying his ride
stopped screeching and started to laugh.

Before coming to land he grabbed hold
with one hand
and from the giraffe's tail he just hung.
This made Jerry jump and cough up the lump
that was blocking the air to his lung.

'Excuse me', he said with a shake of his head, 'you must think me terribly rude. I like a good laugh', said Jerry giraffe 'but NOT when I'm eating my food!'

# The Little Frog

The little frog sat on a stone,
looking sad and all alone.
He looked up and down, left and right,
but there was not another frog in sight.

He stared in the pond
and made a wish.

"I wish that I could have been a fish."

With a whish and whoosh
and a bing bang boo
Suddenly his wish came true.

The little fish swam here and there,
up and down and everywhere.
Always moving, always wet,
trying to avoid the angler's net.
Oh, he thought, a fish's life is so absurd –

"I wish that I could have been a bird."

With a whish and whoosh
and a bing bang boo
Suddenly his wish came true.

The little bird away from his nest,
feathers blown from east to west,
Always searching for some food
to take back to his hungry brood.
Where shall I go, this way or that?

"Oh I wish I could have been a cat."

With a whish and a whoosh
and a bing bang boo
Suddenly his wish came true.

The little cat out for a stroll,
came upon a waterfall.
Frightened of water, now which way to go,
the little cat just didn't know.
Oh there's a creature with all the luck –

"I wish that I could have been a duck."

With a whish and a whoosh
and a bing bang boo
Suddenly his wish came true.

But, the little duck could take no rest
he quickly had to build his nest.
Somewhere secret, out of sight
to keep him safe throughout the night.
He saw something hop onto a log – and thought

"I wish that I could have been a frog."

The little frog sat by a stream,
awake now from his daytime dream.
He shivered at what he had seen,
all the creatures he could have been.

Then hopping and jumping
in the muddy bog,
Happiest of all was the little frog.

# The Songbirds

Little blackbird in the tree
Won't you sing a song for me.
Sing it loud and sing it clear
Sing it for us all to hear.

Little bird, oh little thrush
Hidden in the hawthorn bush
Chest puffed out and beak held high
Please sing your pretty lullaby.

Mother bird up in the nest
I think your song is the best.
Sing your babies off to sleep
And stop their noisy cheep,
cheep, cheep.

Little birds on the wing
Gone now till the early Spring.
Come back soon to us and bring
Your repertoire of songs to sing.

# The Humble Bumblebee

In Summer, when the flowers bloom
I fly inside their little room
And gather nectar hidden there
As only bees and insects dare.
The open flowers welcome me
For I'm the humble bumblebee.

Occasionally, I lose my way
And into open windows stray
And through the clear glass spy the flowers
But now to reach them could take hours.
Oh, I just want to be set free
I'm such a fumbling bumblebee.

Now I never mean to cause alarm
I'd never knowingly do harm
But no matter how hard I try
My buzzing makes the children cry.
Their panicking it frightens me
Then I'm a stumbling bumblebee.

Exhausted on the window sill
I try to hide by keeping still.
I'm caught in a glass and lifted high
And think the time has come to die.
But some brave person sets me free
Oh, I'm the luckiest bumblebee.

# In My Garden

Out in the garden in the flowerbeds
Where the trees sway in the breeze
and flowers shake their heads,
Live ladybirds, butterflies and caterpillars too
Hidden in the undergrowth, camouflaged from view.

Out in the garden in the grass so green
Where beetles scurry in a hurry
not wanting to be seen,
Live wriggly worms and bugs and slugs,
just below the ground
Hidden in the dark wet soil,
they never make a sound.

Out in the garden on the island in the pond
Where flowers are small and reeds grow tall and tadpoles swim around,
The moorhens nest and little ducks rest from learning how to float
Hidden by the rocks and grass, surrounded by their moat.

Out in the garden with friends or on my own
Where I can play and stay all day
and never be alone,
Whilst wriggly worms and
butterflies are watching everywhere
Hidden in my garden, but
I know that they are there.

# The Messages

**Daisy, Dale and Fred** – the importance of friendship and taking care of one another.

**Jerry Giraffe** – taking care when eating not to joke and mess about.

**The Little Frog** – the importance of being happy and contented with what you are and not wanting to be someone else or envious of others.

**The Songbirds** – appreciating things around us and the pleasures that can be found just listening.

**The Humble Bumblebee** – the importance of not giving up in sticky situations because there is always hope.

**In My Garden** – being aware that there are many living things that share our earth and that nature is all around us.

*For my grandchildren*
*Holly, Daniel, Erica, Sammy, Aaron and Miles.*

## About the Author

Ann was a teenager in the 60s but despite this being a time of much social change, in many families it was still considered unimportant for girls to receive anything other than a basic education. This was the situation for Ann who, despite not being allowed to accept her place at Grammar school, went on to become a highly successful businesswoman.

Ann's career led her to becoming a company director and manager of companies which produced entertainment and training using the media of video, computers and broadcast television.

Ann wrote this collection of poems just before she was diagnosed with FTD, a rare form of dementia that can affect people from about forty onwards. Being a degenerative illness, FTD leads to mental incapacity, loss of speech, loss of mobility and, ultimately, complete dependence on palliative care.

Given the advanced stage of Ann's illness, her family have taken on the task of publishing her book and donating proceeds to charitable institutions working in the area of dementia.

In writing the poems, it was Ann's intention to help children appreciate the little things in life that make a difference in how we see the world and conduct our lives. She has achieved this in a light-hearted way by introducing characters and situations that children, from an early age, will relate to and, in so doing, learn about such diverse topics as manners, friendship, envy and nature.

Ann lives with her husband on the south coast of England and has two sons and six grandchildren.